W0006784

When Cultures Meet

John Perritano

PICTURE CREDITS

Cover, pages 2-3, 14, 15, 20-21, 25 (top left), 31 (center left), 34-c, 34-d, 35-b, 35-c © The Granger Collection, NY; title page, page 26 (bottom left) © Werner Forman/Art Resource, NY; title page (inset) © William Mullins; page 4-5 (top and bottom), page 5 (bottom right) © Danny Lehman/Corbis; page 5 (top right), page 32 © Robert Landau/Corbis; page 6-7 © Réunion des Musées Nationaux/Art Resource, NY; page 8, page 25 (top right) © National Geographic Society, All Rights Reserved, Illustration by John Berkey; page 9 © Dave G. Houser/Corbis; page 10 (top left), page 30 (top left), page 34-a © Frederic Didillon/Taxi/Getty Images; page 10 (top right and bottom left), page 29 (bottom) © Royalty-Free/Corbis; page 10 (bottom right) © Lynda Richardson/Corbis; page 11, page 25 (bottom left), page 30 (top right) © Bettman/Corbis; page 12, page 25 (bottom right), page 34-e William Penn's Treaty with the Indians in 1683 (oil on canvas), West, Benjamin (1738-1820) (after) /Friends' House, Euston, London, UK/The Bridgeman Art Library; page 13 (top left) © Tom Stewart/Corbis; page 13 (top right) © Pat Doyle/Corbis; page 13 (bottom left), page 30 (bottom right) © Richard Hamilton Smith/Corbis; page 13 (bottom right) © Ted Grant/Masterfile; page 16-17 © Raymond Gehman/National Geographic Image Collection; page 18 © National Geographic Society, All Rights Reserved, Illustration by Ned M. Siedler; page 19, page 34-b © Kevin R. Morris/Corbis; page 21 © Geoffrey Clements/Corbis; page 22, page 31 (top left) © Corbis; page 23 © Brian A. Vikander/Corbis; page 26-27 © Molly Riley/Reuters/Corbis; page 27 (top right) © Photodisc/Getty Images; page 28 © Nathan Benn/Corbis; page 29 (top) © Paul Almasy/Corbis; page 30 (bottom left) Dale C. Spartus/Corbis; page 31 (top right) © Richard T. Nowitz/Corbis; page 31 (center right) © Chase Swift/ Corbis; page 31 (map), page 35-a Elizabeth Wolf; page 31 (bottom right) David Aubrey/ Corbis; page 33 (left) Expeditions in the Americas, Author Stephen Currie © 2004, cover art George Catlin, La Salle's Party Entering the Mississippi In

Canoes, February 6, 1682 Paul Mellon Collection, Image © 2003 Board of Trustees, National Gallery of Art, Washington, (inset) © Charles & Josette Lenars/Corbis; page 33 (center) Colonial Life, Author Barbara Burt © 2002, cover art The Granger Collection, NY; page 33 (right) Two Cultures Meet, Author Ann Rosi © 2002, cover art Courtesy Library of Congress/ PhotoAssist Inc./Woodfin Camp and Associates, (inset) © The Granger Collection, NY; page 35-d Gunter Marx Photography/Corbis; page 35-e Prairie Indian Encampment, c.1870 (oil on canvas), Stanley, John Mix (1814-72)/© The Detroit Institute of Arts, USA, Gift of Mrs. Blanche Ferry Hooker/The Bridgeman Art Library.

Produced through the worldwide resources of the National Geographic Society, John M. Fahey, Jr., President and Chief Executive Officer; Gilbert M. Grosvenor, Chairman of the Board; Nina D. Hoffman, Executive Vice President and President, Books and Education Publishing Group.

PREPARED BY NATIONAL GEOGRAPHIC SCHOOL PUBLISHING

Ericka Markman, Senior Vice President and President, Children's Books and Education Publishing Group; Steve Mico, Senior Vice President, Editorial Director, Publisher; Francis Downey, Executive Editor; Richard Easby, Editorial Manager; Anne Stone, Lori Dibble Collins, Editors; Bea Jackson, Director of Layout and Design; Jim Hiscott, Design Manager; Cynthia Olson, Art Director; Margaret Sidlosky, Illustrations Director; Matt Wascavage, Manager of Publishing Services; Sean Philpotts, Jane Ponton, Production Managers; Ted Tucker, Production Specialist.

MANUFACTURING AND QUALITY CONTROL

Christopher A. Liedel, Chief Financial Officer; Phillip L. Schlosser, Director; Clifton M. Brown III, Manager.

◀ Europeans traded with
Native Americans.

Contents

CONSULTANT AND REVIEWER
J.M. Opal, Colby College

BOOK DESIGN/PHOTO RESEARCH
Steve Curtis Design, Inc.

Copyright © 2006 National Geographic Society.
All Rights Reserved. Reproduction of the whole or any part of the
contents without written permission from the publisher is prohibited.
National Geographic, National Geographic School Publishing,
National Geographic Reading Expeditions, and the Yellow Border
are registered trademarks of the National Geographic Society.

Published by the National Geographic Society
1145 17th Street N.W.
Washington, D.C. 20036-4688

ISBN-13: 978-0-7922-5455-3

2017 2016 2015 2014 2013
4 5 6 7 8 9 10 11 12 13 14 15

Printed in Mexico

Homes

What Is Culture?

Every group of people lives a certain way. The way a group of people lives is called **culture**. Culture includes many things:

- Homes that people live in
- Clothing that people wear
- Food that people eat
- Religions that people believe in

What happens when people from different cultures mix? Sometimes people get along well. Other times they do not. But when cultures mix, they always change one another.

....
culture – the way of life of a group of people

Food

Clothing

Religion

Two Cultu

Big Idea

Early contact between Native Americans and Europeans changed life in the Americas forever.

Set Purpose

Learn about changes that happened when Europeans came to the Americas.

In the late 1400s, European **explorers** set sail. They were looking for a new **route** to Asia. They landed in North and South America instead.

The Europeans called this land a New World. But it was not new. Native Americans had lived here for thousands of years. Now two cultures shared one land.

....

explorer – a person who travels to little-known places
route – a way to a place

▶ Europeans began to explore the Americas in the late 1400s.

Questions You Will Explore

What did European explorers find when they came to the Americas?

How did the arrival of the Europeans change life in the Americas?

6

res, One Land

▲ Europeans and Native
Americans had different
clothing and habits.

First Contact

Native Americans did not know what to think
of the Europeans when they first met them.
The Europeans dressed differently. They had
very different **customs.**

Some Native Americans welcomed the
Europeans. Others had heard bad things
about the Europeans before meeting them.
These Native Americans were scared.

....

custom – a habit or typical way of doing something

A New Way of Life

The European **settlers** did many things differently than Native Americans. They also had different beliefs. For example, many Native Americans believed that the land belonged to everyone and should be shared. But the Europeans did not believe in sharing land. They took the Native Americans' land. They built farms and towns.

....

settler – a person who moves to an undeveloped area to live

Corn

Tomatoes

Pumpkins

Potatoes

Native Americans Share New Foods

The Native Americans showed the Europeans many things they had never seen before. For example, the Native Americans grew **crops** that were new to the Europeans. Native Americans grew tomatoes, potatoes, pumpkins, and corn. They showed the Europeans how to grow these crops.

....

crop – a plant that is grown to be used

▲ Native Americans taught
the Europeans skills such
as how to paddle a canoe.

Native Americans Teach New Skills

The Native Americans also showed the
Europeans how to do many things. They
showed them the best places to hunt and fish.
They taught them how to paddle a canoe.
Native Americans helped Europeans learn to
survive in their new home.

▲ The Europeans and Native Americans
traded with one another.

Europeans Trade Goods

The Europeans had things the Native Americans
had never seen before. They had metal tools
and guns. The Europeans traded with the Native
Americans. They traded knives, axes, nails, and
guns for animal furs and food.

....

goods – things that are made or grown and then sold

Pigs

Cows

Sheep

Horses

Europeans Bring New Animals

The Europeans brought animals with them to North and South America. They brought pigs, cows, sheep, and horses. Native Americans had never seen these kinds of animals before. The Europeans showed the Native Americans how to care for these animals.

13

▲ Many Native Americans died
  from European diseases.

Europeans Bring Disease

The Europeans also brought diseases with
them when they came to the Americas. Many
Native Americans died from these diseases.
For example, Europeans brought a disease
called **smallpox**. Millions of Native Americans
died from smallpox.

smallpox – a deadly disease that causes sores on the skin

14

▲ Europeans and Native
Americans learned from
one another.

A Changed Life

After the Europeans arrived in the Americas,
life for both cultures was never the same.

Europeans had to get used to life in a new
land. They ate new foods and learned new
ways of fishing and hunting.

For Native Americans, life changed even more.
They had to learn to live with the Europeans.
This meant changing some of their customs
and their culture.

Stop and Think!

How did the arrival
of the Europeans change
life in the Americas?

Closer Look

Recap
Tell how the two cultures changed after meeting one another.

Set Purpose
Look at how the horse changed the way Native Americans lived.

The Horse Comes to America

Before the Europeans came to the Americas, Native Americans traveled on foot. They hunted on foot.

Then one day they saw animals they had never seen before. Those animals were horses. Where had they come from?

The Europeans had brought horses with them to America. Horses changed the way of life for many Native Americans.

Horses in America

Christopher Columbus was the first European to bring horses to America. He brought them in 1492. A few years later, the Spanish introduced horses to Native Americans living in Florida and the Carolinas.

Native Americans living in the West did not see a horse until 1598. That is when Spanish settlers moved to New Mexico. The settlers brought many horses with them.

◀ The Spanish brought horses with them when they came to America.

Learning to Ride

Native Americans watched how Europeans used and treated their horses. Native Americans soon learned how to care for the animals. They also learned how to ride. Native Americans found that using horses made many jobs easier.

▼ Native Americans became skilled at riding horses.

Life Before the Horse

Before horses arrived, Native Americans who lived on the Great Plains lived in villages. Their homes were made out of dirt and clay. During the summer, the men hunted buffalo. Their summer homes were **tepees** made of animal skins.

The men hunted buffalo on foot. Men sneaked up on the buffalo and threw spears at them. Hunters also killed buffalo by chasing them off a cliff. Hunting buffalo was very dangerous.

....
tepee – a tent used by Native Americans

▼ **Before they had horses, Native Americans hunted buffalo by sneaking up on them.**

Life After the Horse

With horses, Native Americans could hunt from horseback. They could also move more easily from place to place. They could follow and hunt buffalo all year. Horses pulled the tepees from camp to camp.

With the horse, hunting took much less time. Native Americans now had free time to do other things. Women spent more time sewing clothes and making jewelry. Men played games. Men also held more religious ceremonies.

▼ **Native Americans learned to hunt on horseback.**

Horse Power

Horses could travel faster than people. They could also go farther and carry heavier loads. With horses, Native Americans had more choices about where to live.

▲ **Native Americans used horses to move their belongings.**

A Changed Culture

The horse allowed Native Americans to go wherever they wanted. Native American **tribes** who had never met now traded with one another. The horse changed the way Native Americans lived.

....

tribe – a group of people or families living together

Stop and Think!

How did the horse change life for Native Americans?

▼ Horses changed the way Native Americans traveled and lived.

Recap
Explain how the horse changed Native American culture.

Set Purpose
Learn more about changes that happened when Europeans came to the Americas.

When Cultures Meet

European explorers came to North and South America in the late 1400s. They found Native Americans living there. The meeting of these two cultures changed life in the Americas forever.

Here are some ideas that you learned about early contact between Europeans and Native Americans.

- European settlers first came to the Americas in the 1400s.
- Native Americans and Europeans had different customs.
- Europeans learned skills from the Native Americans.
- Native Americans and Europeans traded with one another.

Check What You Have Learned

How did the arrival of Europeans change life in the Americas?

▲ In the 1400s, the first Europeans sailed to the Americas.

▲ Europeans and Native Americans had different ways of dressing and living.

▲ Native Americans taught Europeans how to survive in the Americas.

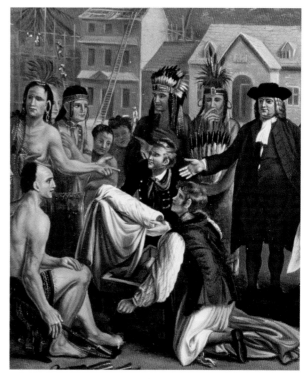

▲ Native Americans and Europeans traded for things such as cloth and metal tools.

A Native American Museum

In 2004, a new museum opened. It is called the National Museum of the American Indian. The museum is part of the Smithsonian Institution in Washington, D.C. It tells the story of Native American culture. There are thousands of objects on display. People come from all over to see the museum. They come to learn about the earliest Americans.

▼ This is a carved box from the museum. It shows a mother seal and her baby.

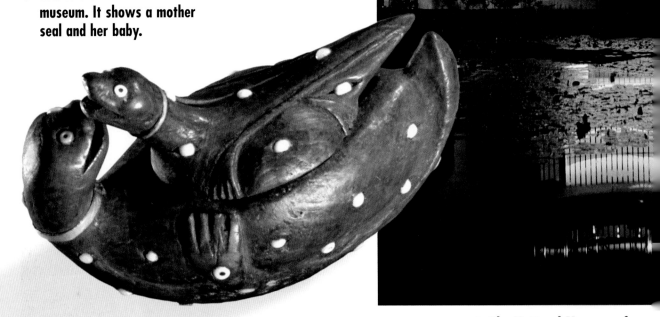

▲ The National Museum of the American Indian

◀ Europeans built missions to teach people about Christianity.

A Different Religion

Native Americans did not follow one religion. Some tribes worshiped animals such as the buffalo. Other tribes worshiped objects in the sky like the sun.

Europeans believed in a religion called Christianity. The Spanish sent missionaries to teach Native Americans about Christianity. The Spanish built missions in California and in other places. Missions were schools and churches.

Many Tribes, Many Cultures

Aztec, Crow, Iroquois, Mohawk, and Mohegan are names of just a few Native American tribes that lived in North America. Each tribe had its own religion, language, and culture. Each had its own way of doing things.

In the Northeast, Native Americans cut down trees to build houses. They also used wood to build canoes and tools. In the deserts of the Southwest, Native Americans built houses of adobe, which is a kind of mud.

▼ An Iroquois man dances and chants outside a traditional longhouse.

► A bowl collects sticky sap from a tree.

Native American Chewing Gum

Do you like chewing gum? Native Americans living in New England introduced the European settlers to spruce sap. Sap is sticky. It comes from trees. The settlers used this sticky sap to make an early form of chewing gum. Today, the average American chews 300 sticks of gum a year.

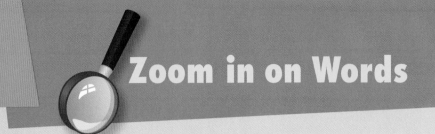

Many kinds of words are used in this book. Here you will learn about words that name things. You will also learn about words that sound alike, but mean different things.

Nouns

A noun is a word that names a person, place, or thing. Look at the sentences below. How many nouns can you find?

Corn was an important crop for Native Americans.

People explored lakes and streams in a **canoe.**

The man used an **ax** to chop down a tree.

Europeans brought **sheep** with them to the Americas.

Homophones

Homophones are words that sound alike, but have different meanings. Find the homophones below. Then write a new sentence for each homophone.

The ships set **sail** for new lands.

Corn is on **sale** at the market.

When people **meet,** they often shake hands.

Native Americans ate deer **meat.**

Explorers wanted to find new trade **routes.**

The **roots** of a plant grow down into the soil.

Research and Write

Write About a New Culture

Learn about the culture in a different country. Find out about customs and traditions in the country you choose. Make a poster showing what you have learned.

Research
Collect books and reference materials, or go online.

Read and Take Notes
As you read, take notes and draw pictures.

Write
Make a poster showing information about the culture in the country you picked.

Read and Compare

Read More About Life in the Americas

Find and read other books about the first contact between Native Americans and Europeans.

- How did Europeans and Native Americans help one another?
- How did life in America change after Europeans arrived?
- Which changes do you think were the most important?

Books to Read

▲ Read about early European explorers who came to North and South America.

▲ Discover the culture of an American community in the 1700s.

▲ See how Native Americans and Europeans helped each other and also clashed.

Glossary

crop (page 10)
A plant that is grown to be used
Corn was an important crop for Native Americans.

KEY CONCEPT

culture (page 4)
The way of life of a group of people
Having horses changed the culture of many Native American tribes.

KEY CONCEPT

custom (page 8)
A habit or typical way of doing something
It was a Native American custom to hunt on foot.

KEY CONCEPT

explorer (page 6)
A person who travels to little-known places
European explorers first came to the Americas in the 1400s.

goods (page 12)
Things that are made or grown and then sold
Europeans traded goods like knives and axes in return for food.

KEY CONCEPT

route (page 6)

A way to a place

The Europeans were looking for a new trade route.

settler (page 9)

A person who moves to an undeveloped area to live

The European settlers learned many things from the Native Americans.

smallpox (page 14)

A deadly disease that causes sores on the skin

Millions of Native Americans died from smallpox.

tepee (page 20)

A tent used by Native Americans

Some Native Americans lived in tepees made of animal skins.

KEY CONCEPT

tribe (page 23)

A group of people or families living together

Each Native American tribe has its own culture and beliefs.

Index